Back in Time

Ancient History for Kids Greek Alphabet and Roman Numerals!

Children's Ancient History Books

Left Brain Kids
Educational Books for Children

 **globe** (GLOHB): A globe is a sphere or ball-shaped model with a map of the Earth printed on it. Globes usually show larger areas of land and water, such as continents and oceans.

 **land** (LAND): The part of the Earth's surface that is not covered by water.

 **map** (MAP): A flat drawing of an area. There are maps of streets, towns, cities, the world, and much more. Maps contain symbols and colors, which all stand for something larger.

Index

Websites to Visit

www.kids.nationalgeographic.com

www.kidsgeo.com/geology-for-kids

www.maps4kids.com

About the Author

Ellen K. Mitten has been teaching four and five year-olds since 1995. She and her family love reading all sorts of books!

In ancient civilizations, each country had to develop its own system, especially for writing and measuring things.

ΑΥΤΟΝΠΡ

ΜΜΑΤΕΒΑΚΑ

ΠΑΝΗΓΥΡΙΑΙ

ΑΩΟΝΕΦΕΥ

ΤΑΡΧΗΝΙΩ

Ancient Greeks had developed a system for writing the alphabet. It was their commonality in writing and language which bound Greeks together.

This alphabet writing has been widely used even until this day.

ΟΝ ΚΑ ΑΠΕ

ΠΑΣ ΑΤΟ

ΔΞΟΝΙ ΕΠΤ

ΗΡΑΚΛΛ ΤΟ

ΠΣΟΦΦΡΟ

ΕΥΦΡΕΣΗ

Most of the Greek alphabet was taken from the Phoenician alphabet, although they had to add a few letters.

The Greeks also assigned vowel sounds to some letters of the Greek alphabet.

no · ɒ · ... hen...

EBR̄ · ø · henrr...

⁊ ꝑpoꝭ ⁊ honoꝛ...

ac · CAPPELLA

IS · PREBENO...

VE · DEDICAT

n · TVLLEN · in

...CAT · EODE

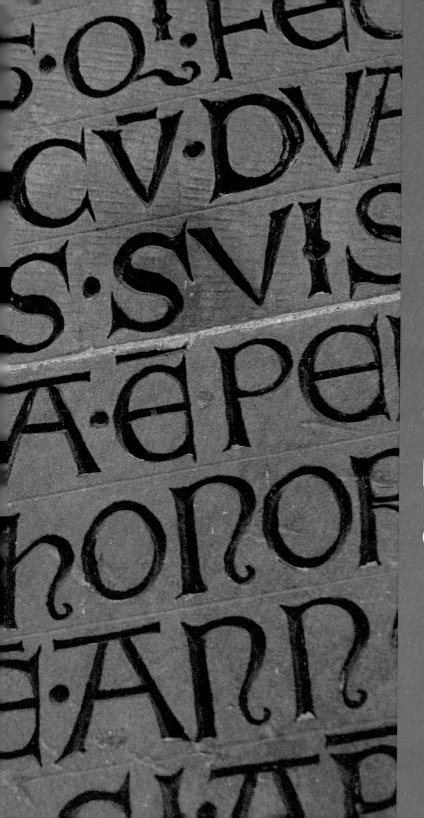

Alpha, beta, and omega are among the 24 letters in Greek alphabet.

These Greek letters had been used also to write Greek numerals.

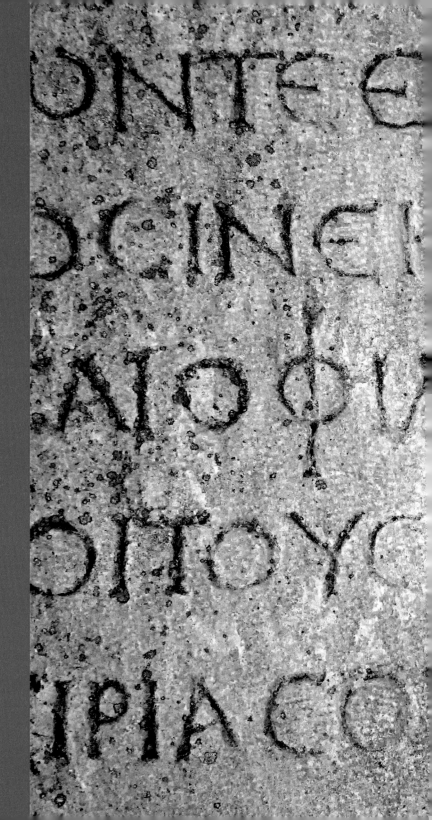

ΖΟΥCΙΑΝΑΥΤ

ΤΗCCΕΠΙΦΑΝΟ

ΟΥCΙΝΑΥΞΕCC

ΟΙΟΥΤΟΥCΙΠ

ΟΥ̣Ι̣Ρ̣ΕΙCΡΟ

ΜΟΝΔΔΗΙΑΣΟΣΚΟΛΛΥΤΕ   ΣΠΕ
ΛΥΝΑΙΚΑΕΙΕΡΑΙΣΠΡΟΣΜΕ   ΗΗΚ
ΚΕΔΔΔ ΚΕΦΑΛΑΙΟΝΗΑ   ΔΔΙ   ΙΑΙ
ΤΟΠΟΙΚΟΧΧΧΗΗΗΔΠ ΙΕ   ΙΑΙ
ΧΙΗΗΗΗΓΣΗΑΝΑΛΟΜΑΤΟΑ   ΣΑ
ΗΕΠΙΤΕΣΠΑΝΔΙ   ΜΙ
ΧΑΛΔΟΕΣΠΡΥΤΑΝΕΥΟΥΣ   ΔΔ
ΜΑΤΑΓΑΡΑΤΑΜΙΟΝΤΕΣ
ΕΣΑΙΧΜΟΗΑΛΡΥΙΕΘΕΝ
ΔΟΧΟΝΙ   ΧΗΗΔΔΔΠΗΗ   ΗΗ
ΝΑΛΟΜΑΤΑΗΟΝΕΜΑΤΑΣΑ
ΔΥΟΗΕΣΑΣΤΟΝΛΟΛΟΝΗΑ   ΧΑΡ
ΦΟ ΓΝΔΡΑΧΜΕΣΗΕΚΑΤΕ   ΑΤΔΔ
ΚΕ ΔΙΟΝΗΟΝΕΜΑΤΟΝ   ΕΝΗΔ
ΟΡΛΙΚΟΡΑΒΔΟΣΕΟΣΤΟΝ   ΗΗΧΡΥ
ΝΤΟΝΠΡΟΣΕΟΤΟΝΚΑΤΑΤ   ΧΑΛ
ΟΝΤΟΝΤΡΙΤΟΝΗΑΠΟΤ Β   ΣΗΕΚΑ
ΣΔΙΟΝΕΣΗΑΜΕΝΙΝΙΑΔΕΣ   ΟΝΙΔ
ΝΕΗΟΥΚΟΝΔΠΗΗΗΑ   ΣΧ

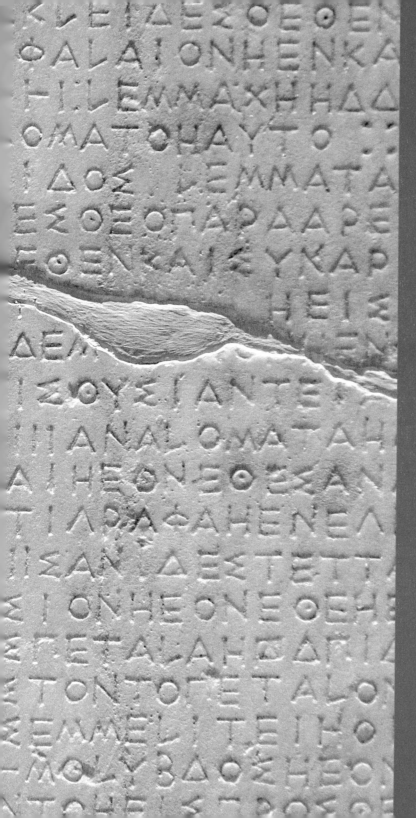

Some of these Greek letters are used in the fields of Science and Mathematics.

The first Greek alphabet didn't have upper and lower case letters.

...ΠΗ.ΕΠΙΚΑΛΑ.ΠΠΟCΤΥΚΥ...ΘΚΙΝΕ
ΜΟΙΕΝΟΜΟΥΕ.ΕΡΟΥCΕΠΙΡΑ
.ΕΠΙ.ΙΕΟΥΡΑΝΙΟΥΦΡΟΝΤΙΑ
ΚΑΘΙΔΡΥCΕΛΕΧΑΡΑΚΤΗΡΕΙ
.ΜΑΤΩΝΕΙΚΟCΙΝΑΘΩΜΑΤΟΥ.
ΟΝΕΥΠΟΙΑΗΤΙCΕΜΗCΥΧΗ.
ΔΟΜΩΝΕΝΕΛΑΤΑΚΛΕΙCΤΟΙCΠ.
.ΝΙC.ΛΕCΩΜΑΤΟCΠΗΡΛΙΚΟΥΠΡΟΦ
ΕΠΙΝΟΙΕCΠΙΟΤΑΛΛΑΙΟΥ.ΘΕΟΛΙΛ.
ΛΕΙΟ.ΙΠΡΟΝΑ.ΝΕΗΚΟΝΕΚ.
ΞΕΛΥΤΙ.ΕΕΙ.ΡΑΓΟ..ΛΗΛΑΤΟ.
.ΗΠΕΙΧΛΑΛ.ΤΗΡΑ..ΕΤΗΕΩ
..ΕΝΑΥΤΟΝ.ΩΤ.

The Ancient Greeks' writing of letters and numbers paved the way for them to develop and excel in the field of literature.

Ancient Greeks understood having these systems would greatly help them in making a mark in the worlds history.

The Roman Numeral was the only written numbering system used in Ancient Rome.

Roman Numerals do not have a zero and have 7 digits only.

Symbol	Value
I	1
V	5
X	10
L	50
C	100
D	500
M	1,000

Roman numbers are formed by adding the values, i.e II is (2) and XI is (11).

Roman Numerals were used for counting the number of objects and also the order of people that has the same name (Henry I, Henry II, Henry III, Henry IV).

Roman numerals were also used for writing on cornerstones of buildings to show the origin of a building.

Roman numerals are a combination of letters from the Latin alphabet.

Did you enjoy reading? Now share this to your friends.

AEDE[...]

RIS · MAGN[...] SINE [...]

[...] REFECI · [...] REFECI · ET · A[...]

NTES · REFECI [...] IVLIVM ·

FORVM · IVLIVM [...] OP

[...]OFLIGATAQVE · SVB

EIVS · SOLO · HEREDIBVS ·

CI · AB · HERE[...]

[...]ITATE · SENATVS

[...] FLAMINIA[...]

[...] SO[...]

Made in the USA
San Bernardino, CA
17 April 2019

Solving Problems at the Zoo

Nellie Wilder

Smithsonian

Consultants

Jen Zoon
Communications Specialist
Office of Communications
Smithsonian National Zoo

Amy Zoque
STEM Coordinator and Instructional Coach
Vineyard STEM School
Ontario Montclair School District

Publishing Credits

Rachelle Cracchiolo, M.S.Ed., *Publisher*
Conni Medina, M.A.Ed., *Editor in Chief*
Diana Kenney, M.A.Ed., NBCT, *Series Developer*
Emily R. Smith, M.A.Ed., *Content Director*
Véronique Bos, *Creative Director*
Robin Erickson, *Art Director*
Michelle Jovin, M.A., *Associate Editor*
Mindy Duits, *Series Designer*
Lee Aucoin, *Senior Graphic Designer*
Smithsonian Science Education Center

Image Credits: front cover, p.1, © Smithsonian (photo by Mehgan Murphy); pp.4–12, p.13 (top), p.14 (bottom), p.15, p.16, p.17 (bottom), p.18, p.19, p.22 (top), p.23 (top) © Smithsonian; all other images from iStock and/or Shutterstock.

Library of Congress Cataloging-in-Publication Data

Names: Rice, Dona, author. | Smithsonian Institution, author.
Title: Solving problems as the zoo / Dona Herweck Rice, Smithsonian.
Description: Huntington Beach, CA : Teacher Created Materials, [2020] |
  Audience: K to Grade 3. |
Identifiers: LCCN 2018049793 (print) | LCCN 2018050706 (ebook) | ISBN
  9781493868971 (eBook) | ISBN 9781493866571 (paperback)
Subjects: LCSH: Zoo keepers--Washinton (D.C.)--Juvenile literature. |
  National Zoological Park (U.S.)
Classification: LCC QL50.5 (ebook) | LCC QL50.5 .R53 2020 (print) | DDC
  590.73/753--dc23
LC record available at https://lccn.loc.gov/2018049793

☼ Smithsonian

Teacher Created Materials

5301 Oceanus Drive
Huntington Beach, CA 92649-1030
www.tcmpub.com
ISBN 978-1-4938-6657-1

Table of Contents

All in a Day's Work

Life at the Smithsonian's National Zoo is fun! **Keepers** work hard to make it that way.

Keepers gave this tiger a ball to play with.

Bear cubs play at the
Smithsonian's National Zoo.

Keepers take care of animals. They feed them. They keep them safe. Keepers also make sure animals have fun!

A keeper brushes an ape's teeth.

A keeper gives an alpaca treats while the alpaca paints.

A keeper trains lemurs to stand so she can study them.

Making It Work

Keepers face problems each day. They must find the best ways to do their work.

A keeper measures meals for different animals.

A keeper trains a goat to touch a ball so she can check the goat.

Checking Henderson the monkey can be tough. But keepers trained him to come when he sees a ball. That is how keepers talk to him.

A keeper gives Henderson a strawberry as a treat for coming.

Just Right

Temperature in a fish tank must be just right. It is checked first thing each day. Animals can get sick if it is too high or too low.

Keepers also check the birds. They hit a wood block to call them. The sound means breakfast time!

Keepers mix fruit and worms for birds to eat.

A keeper notes which birds come to her after she hits a wood block.

Checking fish can be hard. Adding **medicine** to the water helps. It makes the fish go to sleep.

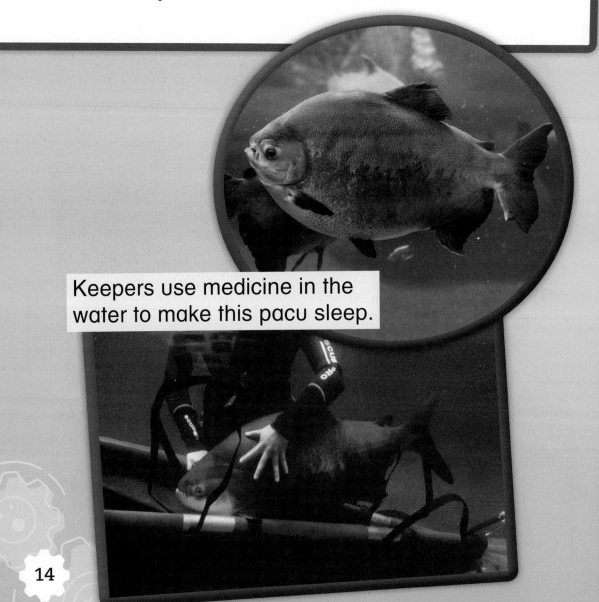

Keepers use medicine in the water to make this pacu sleep.

These are arapaima fish, like the one put in a tube.

A Fishy Problem

In 2015, keepers had to help a big fish. The fish could hurt them. So, keepers cut slots in a tube. The fish stayed in the tube while they worked on it.

Feeding the animals is a big job! Each has its own foods and **schedule**. Keepers must know them all.

A keeper ties vegetables to wood so the food will sink for the fish.

Zap!

Electric eels may look smooth and soft. But these fish can **shock** keepers! Keepers wear gloves when feeding eels. These special gloves protect keepers from harm.

Big Job

It is a big job to be a good keeper. But the rewards are bigger!

Keepers check the health of a fishing cat kitten.

A keeper rewards alpacas with carrot slices.

STEAM CHALLENGE

The Problem

You and your friend have new jobs at the zoo. You must feed a bird called a finch. Your task is to make a bird-feeding hat. One of you will wear the hat while the other checks the bird!

The Goals

- Design a hat you can wear so that it holds one big spoonful of bird food.
- Design a place on your hat for the finch to land and eat.
- Design a strong enough hat to hold both the bird feed and a coin to represent the finch.

Research and Brainstorm

What do finches eat? How much does a finch weigh? What coin is about that same weight?

Design and Build

Draw your plan. How will it work? What materials will you use? Make your bird-feeding hat!

Test and Improve

Put bird feed in the hat. Add the coin. Does it hold? Does anything fall? Can you make it better? Try again.

Reflect and Share

How many finches could you feed on your hat at one time? Is there something else you could make that would be better for feeding and checking a finch?

Glossary

keepers

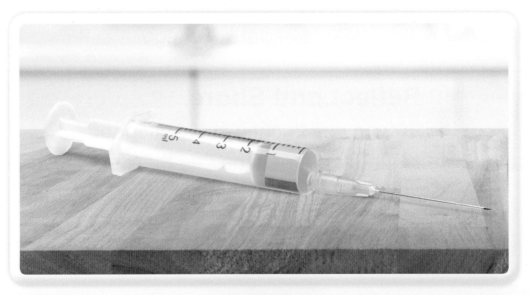

medicine

schedule

shock

temperature

Career Advice
from Smithsonian

Do you want to be a keeper? Here are some tips to get you started.

"To be a great keeper you have to be curious. You have to work hard and study too."
— *Ashton Ball, Small Mammal House Keeper*

" When I was young, I fell in love with orangutans. I wanted to teach people about them and how we can save them. So I studied to be a keeper!"
— *Kara Ingraham, Small Mammal House Keeper*